YOUR KNOWLEDGE HAS VALUE

Nick Birch

Birth of the Backyard Business

The Impact of Technology on Creative Industries

GRIN Verlag

Bibliografische Information der Deutschen Nationalbibliothek:

Die Deutsche Bibliothek verzeichnet diese Publikation in der Deutschen National-
bibliografie; detaillierte bibliografische Daten sind im Internet über http://dnb.d-
nb.de/ abrufbar.

Imprint:

Copyright © 2009 GRIN Verlag GmbH
Druck und Bindung: Books on Demand GmbH, Norderstedt Germany
ISBN: 978-3-656-60778-6

This book at GRIN:

http://www.grin.com/en/e-book/269614/birth-of-the-backyard-business

GRIN - Your knowledge has value

Der GRIN Verlag publiziert seit 1998 wissenschaftliche Arbeiten von Studenten, Hochschullehrern und anderen Akademikern als eBook und gedrucktes Buch. Die Verlagswebsite www.grin.com ist die ideale Plattform zur Veröffentlichung von Hausarbeiten, Abschlussarbeiten, wissenschaftlichen Aufsätzen, Dissertationen und Fachbüchern.

Visit us on the internet:

http://www.grin.com/

http://www.facebook.com/grincom

http://www.twitter.com/grin_com

BIRTH OF THE BACKYARD BUSINESS

The Impact of Technology on Creative Industries

Nick Birch 2009

Technology is evolving faster than we can shake an iPod at, and like a frenetic silhouette on a primary-coloured backdrop it is difficult to see the entire picture – you are only left with a gist of what on earth is actually going on, a feeling that you want to jump up and be a part of it. Even though it helps to analyse the progress of technology in the creative fields historically, it still remains implausible to predict exactly where it will take us even in the near future. The film, television and music industries are an interesting source to start with where we may begin to understand some of the ways technology is not only enhancing the ability to create more, but also the way it affects the way business is performed.

The late-nineties and early millennia saw a profound change in the way creative industries operate. It's pertinent to realise that while technology has been enhancing the creative industries to no end, in fact, to the point of fear, the creative industries have in turn been demanding the enhancement of technology. And what is the greatest demand of all? Price.

Technologies designed for creative industries have all kinds of domino effects on other technologies used in different sectors. The advent of digital High-Definition gave filmmakers a cheaper and very competitive alternative to using film (Lantz 2009), instead using digital tape rather than enduring the processes of film and everything that entails. Expensive stock, developing, the time-consuming process of telecine where the film is transferred to digital tape, scratches and dirt removed and finally colour-graded all for an hourly rate that would make a law firm blush. Even better, since what has been shot is already in digital format, filmmakers such as George Lucas could then shoot with metadata making it easier for the graphic artists to add their effects (Scan 2003, p.4) (Bennet 2003). This was also great news for smaller productions on a budget. Now cameras are capturing images as files rather than tape, such as the Panasonic P2 (VideoCraft 2009) and Sony XDCAM (Scan 2004, p.9). Editing system manufacturers such as Avid, a self-proclaimed 'worldwide leader in tools for film and video' (Avid n.d.), have barely had time to catch up with this rapidly evolving technology, with a newer version of the software being released almost before the last. Avid are dropping the hardware and bundling more into software only products (Adcock 2009) in a desperate bid to keep up with their competition (Morris 2009) (JamieG 2009). Companies like Final Cut Pro (Apple) and Adobe have exploited what technology can make possible and made it available for a fraction of the price of what Avid has in the past, forcing Avid to swim along or sink away unless a swift reaction was mobilised.

Technology is becoming cheaper because it is disappearing! Or rather just shrinking from view. Where once you would walk into a post-production house and see a myriad of hardware covering the entire wall of an editing suite, you now have a laptop. A single computer doing everything, it's all now encased in the software as opposed to big, bulky boxes. But that used to be a selling point to customers. Walking into a room full of flashing lights and beeping machines made them feel great about shelling out tens to hundreds of thousands of dollars because let's face it – where else could you gain access to such technology? There weren't too many people with this sheer amount of hardware in their bedrooms. But because technology has made things smaller, doesn't mean it's less impressive. In fact, the creation of more and more powerful computers not only means that you can achieve boundlessly superior results in comparison to yesterday's hardware-based videotape factories, it also means that the need for an operator is diminishing, as is the need for their assistant or the tech who keeps it all working. The technology to do more is now available for less. Much less. So much so that some customers of the film and television industry are buying their own cameras and edit suites for the cost of producing one of their commercials. Does that mean that the new kid who has joined the customer's marketing department who dabbles in home-movies can create better quality commercials than that of a professional production company? It doesn't matter, that customer is gone. Gone away to do it all by themselves. So hasn't technology just performed a profound disservice to this creative industry?

The advancement of technology here has spawned small "backyard" companies who can undercut the prices of bigger production companies due to lower overheads. Clients are now even doing it themselves, without the lattes and plush furniture. But one thing may be missing from this new-found ability to DIY...

Talent.

Just because you can now purchase and cart around all the tools in one box (Monton 2005, p. 8), doesn't mean you can perform like a professional creative. A feature story on the Australian Film Commission (2007) claims that some negatives of DIY vs. facilities editing is that 'you lose the power of a facility 'package deal'' Creative industries have seen the idea of "convergence" emerge as a selling point to their customers. A one-stop-shop where every aspect of the product or project can be performed under the one roof. The AFC has left out a major component from its list of cons and that is the question of talent. Now that you can provide the goods to yourself, can you provide the service? I am sure that was tucked into the price tag somewhere when you went to the production company. So even though now that Final Cut Pro can 'present an exciting alternative for post-production on a low-budget' (Australian Film Commission 2007), who's going to edit the video? Sounds like just because you can buy your own brush and trestle means you can become a great painter. The operative words being "can become" and that's what technology has allowed – the possibility. The means but not the ends. This has not done a disservice to the creative industries, it has merely changed it. But isn't that what technology is supposed to do?

We all know and are well versed in the constantly changing, dynamic wonder known as the internet, with its boundless opportunities that it affords the least likely buccaneers to become the most lucrative of moguls. It has been met with fear by many, something that breaches copyright and steals money away from music record labels and film and television distributers. But while some were worrying about protecting intellectual property rights, others were making squillions through innovation. In a publication on high-tech industries in the UK from The Economic and Social Research Council, it is claimed that Professor Simon Frith of Stirling University asked 'why should an industry whose way of making money was essentially formed in the late 1930s be exempt from the possibilities that there are going to be different ways of making money out of music because of technological change?' (Economic and Social Research Council UK 2004) Well, they shouldn't – not if they're smart. Like video production companies and creative tool manufacturers they are gradually biting the bullet and providing their goods for less. Because technology can make it happen and because the world demands it. And because more is able to be provided, more is demanded. Like shooting and ingesting hours of footage, editing it and providing it to be screened at an event all in the very same day, customers paying for this service come to expect it and eventually ask: what more can be done and for how much less? The internet means we can basically access whatever we want, whenever we want. But what do we want? And is it really what we wanted? Well, we can watch what we want on internet TV, BitTorrent this, Hulu that. Leave comment number 156,009 on a YouTube video, telling the owner just how awful we thought it was. Now why would we do that? Because we *can* and because it really *was* quite awful. Maybe there is a reason behind the grave misfortune that found us stumbling upon such mediocre entertainment.

So the internet has opened up the world of media creation in many industries. In a recent article, McGreal (2009) discusses the effects of cheap and abundant commodities:

> *If anyone can publish a blog that costs almost nothing to operate, you no longer need professional gatekeepers to decide who gets published and who doesn't. In short, the cost of "failure" - of producing content that hardly anyone wants to read - has collapsed, and so we can afford the luxury of widespread "failure"*
>
> *(McGreal 2009)*

This "failure" is then described as resulting in the "amateurisation" of writing and making music. With an enormous audience and an abundance of product, anyone can do anything and no-one can stop it. With this grotesque amount of poor content available, it became important to 'publish, then filter' (McGreal 2009) - enter Google, winning the popularity contest. So surely there is still room for talent in the creative industries? It's wonderful that everybody can write their blogs and peddle their tunes, but there still seems to be a need, a desire for quality stuff. And when it is found, it can spread like a mortally aggressive virus. Distribution for profit may have disintegrated, but what is left in that half-full glass?

Where the internet and file sharing technology has negatively affected the film and music industries through threats to copyright protection, alternative means of distribution have been sought. So you can download your favourite song from iTunes for fewer than two dollars, resting assured of its superior data-rate. If people can obtain the same thing from the same place for free, you'd better make it as close to free as you can and sell it on its quality. The Economic and Social Research Council publication goes on to say that 'as Simon Frith observed, musicians will not stop making music because of the absence of copyright protection' and that 'technology is influencing musical creativity in a far more complex way than is suggested by simply focusing on the production and sale of records' (Economic and

Social Research Council UK 2004). But it is even more interesting to see how technology is affecting the business side of the music industry. For example, with the advent of places like MySpace, artists shared their music with the world simply for that pleasure alone. What many now realise is that they are performing the necessary ground work for the record companies and that artists themselves through their own online publicity have become one of the new business models that the publications (Economic and Social Research Council UK 2004) claims there is a need for. It has never been easier to exploit your band or to create a fan-base, where before the internet you had to travel and perform at as many venues as you could; now you just upload your latest song, RSS feed your fans, twitter away, sit back and watch the hits pile up. Before you know it, you are a backyard business, selling your music or concert tickets online. Enter the record company's talent scout and the band or artist no longer had to be at the right place at the right time, they just needed to create proof of popularity. A new way of doing business is born: MySpace Music, the joint venture with the major record labels was created more than ten months ago (McCarthy 2009) and has of course been suffering its share of doubts and opinions ever since and will probably do so until it is replaced by the next big thing.

So which is it? Is technology enhancing the creative industries or are the creatives telling technology what to do? Where there is a need or a void, it certainly seems to eventually become filled, no matter who is kicking and screaming. Even when it's the creatives who have demanded access to the technology that ends up hurting their profession.

But that's okay. Because their bosses will make them find new and innovative ways to exploit it. And make squillions.

REFERENCES

Adcock, Gary. (2009). *Review: Avid Media Composer 3.0*. Available: http://www.macworld.com.au/reviews/view/review-avid-media-composer-3-0-1589. Last accessed 03 August 2009.

Australian Film Commission. (2007). *The Pros and Cons of DIY vs. Facilities Editing*. Available: http://www.afc.gov.au/newsandevents/afcnews/feature/finalcut/newspage_322.aspx. Last accessed 02 August 2009.

Avid. (n.d.). *Avid Customers React to New Products*. Available: http://www.avid-australia.com.au/company/press/generic_intl_press.asp?taxID=4354. Last accessed 03 August 2009.

Bennett, Bill. (2003). *Is 35mm film dead?* Available: http://www.theage.com.au/articles/2003/02/21/1045638480193.html. Last accessed 02 August 2009.

Economic and Social Research Council UK (2004). Creativity, Technology and the UK's Creative Industries: Where Next? Available: http://www.esrc.ac.uk/ESRCInfoCentre/Images/hi_tech_singles_tcm6-1796.pdf. Last accessed 25 July 2009.

JamieG Analysis. (2009). *Avid is Getting Desperate*. Available: http://www.crafted.com.au/blog/2009/03/07/avid-is-getting-desperate/. Last accessed 03 August 2009.

Lantz, Steve. (2009). *HD Vs Film - The Great Debate*. Available: http://ezinearticles.com/?HD-Vs-Film---The-Great-Debate&id=2451319. Last accessed 02 August 2009.

McCarthy, Caroline. (2009). *Catching up with MySpace Music.* Available: http://news.cnet.com/8301-13577_3-10194538-36.html. Last accessed 03 August 2009.

McGreal, Ryan. (2009). *The Future of Creative Industries: Openness and Abundance or Innovation-Killing Legal Monopolies?* Available: http://www.raisethehammer.org/index.asp?id=911. Last accessed 02 August 2009.

Monton, Vincent. (2005). *Australian Film Commission Fellowship.* Available: http://www.afc.gov.au/downloads/pubs/monton_fellowship.pdf. Last accessed 02 August 2009.

Morris, James. (2009). *Avid Media Composer 3.5.* Available: http://www.goodgearguide.com.au/review/digital_video/avid/media_composer_3_5/300281. Last accessed 03 August 2009.

Scan. (2003). *Star Wars 'The Force' of Sony's New HD System is with George Lucas.* Available: http://www.sony.com.au/objects/pdf/SCAN_Issue3_03.pdf. Last accessed 02 August 2009.

Scan. (2004). *Your Chance to Discover... The XDCAM Professional Disc System.* Available: http://www.sony.com.au/objects/pdf/SCANIssue1_20041.pdf. Last accessed 02 August 2009.

VideoCraft. (2009). *Panasonic Unveils Dramatically Lower Cost P2 Solid-State Memory Card Line.* Available: http://www.videocraft.com.au/plugins/newsfeed.cgi?rm=content&plugin_data_id=27379. Last accessed 03 August 2009.